THE PANIC R

THE PANIC ROOM

POEMS

REBECCA PĂPUCARU

NIGHTWOOD EDITIONS

2017

Nightwood Editions
P.O. Box 1779
Gibsons, BC VON 1V0
Canada
www.nightwoodeditions.com

COVER DESIGN & TYPOGRAPHY: Carleton Wilson

Canada

Canada Council   Conseil des Arts .
for the Arts   du Canada

BRITISH COLUMBIA
ARTS COUNCIL
An agency of the Province of British Columbia

Nightwood Editions acknowledges financial support from
the Government of Canada through the Canada Book Fund and
the Canada Council for the Arts, and from the Province of British Columbia
through the British Columbia Arts Council and the Book Publisher's Tax Credit.

This book has been produced on 100% post-consumer recycled,
ancient-forest-free paper, processed chlorine-free
and printed with vegetable-based dyes.

Printed and bound in Canada.

CIP data available from Library and Archives Canada.

ISBN 978-0-88971-338-3

Family and friends, past and present, near and far.

CONTENTS

WAIT IN THE CAR

WISH YOU WERE HERE

RETOUCHED

WAIT IN
THE CAR

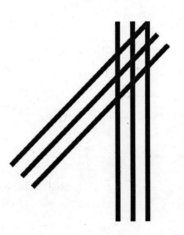

MY ANNE

I pass the workday in throes of Dadaist delight,
processing parental worry at a children's toy factory.
Dear Sirs, My Anne is Barbara Jones. At last, a puzzle all my own,
one with no sharp edges. *Thank you for your email.*
While not intended to be ingested, our Alphabet Cubes
are non-toxic. Sincerely, Rebecca.

Why not, Ms. Păpucaru? Four black cats play among
the consonants of the name I nearly lost to assimilation:
otiose, two round their backs; their fellows sit in cross-section,
Brancusi-sculpted. Second-generation, I'm ignorant of why
the first must balance that dish of milk on its head.
But just listen: *Au, au!* That's Balkan birdsong.

Papa still won't allow his heirs to speak our cursed name.
Still, I exploit his sad air without shame, feeling
like a blasted fraud when I'm called to the stage.
I'm monosyllabic, dark, not some cobbler of laced felt
slippers prized by Black Sea rustics. These days
I'm the right age for childish word games. Barbara, *Greek,*

meaning strange; Anne, *Hebrew, grace.* Eleven words, loosely
translated: *My grace lies in my strangeness to you, and to me.*

BODYBAG

So much depends
on what's in the window
of BODYBAG, the new
fast-fashion store
I pass each morning
on my way to work.

So much depends
on a lawn-green skirt
and sheer floral blouse;
a pair of olive work pants
paired with a tube top.

At the office, I make a point
at least once a day
to bow north. Northeast
to be exact, where the young
girls at BODYBAG pair
a cobalt-blue T with a pair
of sequined shorts.

Another girl readies
the clearance racks for my
Sunday reprieve of unsold
duds from the landfill.
(So much will depend
on a simple taupe shift
I will pick, all good lines,
not a false note in it.)

At the office, I make it a point
at least once a day
to bow north. I bend at the waist
and face northeast.
I don't know where Mecca
begins or ends but I can embrace
a marked-down trend that,
like us, won't survive
next season.

Unless we skirt famine
by mastering photosynthesis,
our post-human skin
changing colour and print
faster than H&M—
then, and only then,
will we laugh at the anachronism
dry cleaning has become,
telling anyone who'll listen:
All of my shoes are hybrids.

COTTAGE COUNTRY

Papa sends me to cottage country
with six new toothbrushes;
himself thirteen when first furnished
with one at a DP camp in Germany
run by Jewish Relief.
Pre-pubescent, I was yet to break
a bone, my body still cushioned
by puppy fat. Not a single scar or cavity.
My teeth were an affront to evil,
my smile whiter than that of any

Pepsodent twin. Freshly minted, integral.
I didn't know how to ski or the names
of trees, Latin or vulgar. I stayed indoors
alone reading comics, wary of avalanches,
of sitting too close to the hearth
and singeing my lashes off. I lost
at Scrabble, was shy at the table.
My friend's parents called me *anti-social*.
Nothing more was ever asked of me
than my presence, much less the art

of dinner-table conversation.
Back home, I surveyed my congregation
of one with the third eye daubed
on my brow, feet reaching for the ground,
my elbows on the table. While I ate,
Papa recalled the woods beyond the camp.
One time he came upon a skating party.
He couldn't believe his luck: food,
blankets and boots, worn but fur-lined.
He can still taste their wine.

MATCHMAKER

The girls were talking childhood fears and I said *beards*. My mother had to write the CBC when Mr. Dressup briefly had one. When he asked what we kids thought was in his Tickle Trunk, I believed it was his previous, clean-shaven face. It was the seventies; men had sideburns, moustaches, full mutton chops. *Plus ça change*. Ladies, I revere the man who chooses bees over stubble, for he makes my task easy. Ladies, don't despair; we'll try the next parish. The one with the mill.

PREVENTION

My father drives from his end of the island to mine, bearing an article establishing a link between soy and breast cancer. Without a word, still wearing his coat, shoulders heavy with snow, he goes for my fridge.

"Death has a life of its own," he says.

What is my father made of these days? As he floods his body with phytochemicals, flavonoids and antioxidants? Bricks of dark chocolate to soften arteries, fistfuls of walnuts to elasticize blood vessels, gallons of pomegranate juice to put down cellular mutiny?

My father calls this his medicine. Taken with the same pleasure as an Aspirin. Overwhelming his body with mixed messages. I can relate. His concern tends to feel like punishment. Leading you to find comfort in the dimpled arms of semi-solids.

But never full rebellion. That only occurs to children who don't take the time, at least once a day, to scare themselves shitless.

I am thinking about snow angels, a grown woman watching her father pour Soy Dream down her sink. Mine always resembled the imprints of stroke victims. Lying in the snow, I flapped my wings until my shoulders ached.

Inside the house, a forty-year-old man with two teenaged daughters consoles himself with a brick of halvah.

WITHOUT PREJUDICE

Another day spent scanning emails
from frantic parents. Subject line:
THIS TOY IS DEFENCTIVE!!!
They attach photos of fluids they suspect
are toxic, evidence I'm under orders
to ignore. My First Nail Art Salon
weeps napalm. A cracked Etch-a-Sketch

knock-off has been double-bagged
and is on its way to our lab.
Conspiracy theories about chemicals
and developmental delays now hold water.
The in-house lawyer has enjoined
me to begin every standard answer
with the shibboleth: *Without prejudice.*

The factory's front is blank concrete.
I enter through a side door. At lunch time
I find doll parts in the microwave:
a measuring cup of fondued limbs, one
hand gripping the glass lip; a head, crying
its features off to a soft, hairless apricot.

The only employee without a car, I take
the bus to the metro. The #115 makes
a complete circuit of the park and its residents—
makers of pharmaceuticals and industrial
solvents. Men in cast-off ski jackets,
stripped of tickets proving the wearer
can afford conveyance up mountains,

hasten from the factories to meet the bus.
A sprawl of lunch boxes on their knees
while I balance this season's purse.
They call to each other in Spanish;
occasionally, one smiles at me;
I bring out my paper. *Endangered seals*
eating endangered salmon.

The bus stops across the street
from the station, a block from the cross
walk: a death trek in winter. I jaywalk
along with the men across two lanes
of rush-hour traffic. Only I know,
it's not the cold that kills, but what
a body must do to stay warm.

ON WATCHING AN EASTERN BLOC COMEDY

It's hard to pull off, a getaway in a Lada.
Mud road. Sudden appearance of a goat. I'm one
generation apart from all this, and ashamed

of my father before his refrigerator, mourning age
spots on lettuce. Our lecturer calls it brilliant,
the late director's parsimonious use of film stock.

He has made a pot-au-feu from onion skins.
Would he call my father a genius? In undershirt
and slippers, hunched over the sink, rescuing

bell peppers for soup stock, muttering,
Still good, gott in himmel, still good.

THE PANIC ROOM (GLUE EAR AT FORTY-FIVE)

The nurse peers inside my right ear:
fluid trapped there, inside the canal,
turning my skull into a Bridge of Sighs

only I can hear. Some seaside bully
has sealed shut my ear with wet sand.
I try not to shout when I speak,

chew gum all day like a bad actor.
I pinch my nostrils shut with thumb
and finger, exhale for the decreed ten

to fifteen seconds. Comes the crackle
of fat in a distant skillet, but no relief.
Through the padded wall of a panic room

my voice reaches me. My good ear?
Unappreciated, unsung and besieged,
like the one son who visits me faithfully:

You'll turn your back on me, too, one day.
Oh, ma, he says, slicing into the birthday
cake he's brought me. *We all will.*

LOBSTER DINNER

How my father loved watching me
at the table. A contest: could I pick
out every scrap from the carapace,
a surgeon unaided? He'd demonstrated
the basics; at eleven I could go it alone.

I went to work with my tools: nut crackers,
two-tined fork. Like at Passover Seder,
each item before me mattered: the Wet-Nap
for my *trayf* hands, lemon-scented;
the bib, emblazoned with a cheery cartoon

of the brute I would soon devour,
waving its crushing claw in greeting. *Wear
it in good health,* Father said. Breathe deep,
then wrench the claws off the trunk (one hand
grasps thorax as the other hand wrestles).

Off with the tail; now the legs: suck up all ten
like wee coral bagpipes plump with gristle.
Quarter both goons, Pincer and Crusher,
at their joints. Pluck the flaps, those spiny
rose petals, off the fin. Find the smallest

entrance on the mangled tail; ease finger
in and push meat out, intact (*Turn your head
and cough*, Father said). That ball
of red snot in the cavity couldn't put me off
my repast. I ate the proof my arthropod,

too, was a girl. I can't undo the wrong
I've done; still, I reverse the home movie,
watch as I blow life into legs with oiled lips,
join tail flaps like stucco tiles. From my mouth
an empty fork issues bearing tissue

from my insides to bolster my Golem.
I attach tail, legs and claws to trunk with gusto;
the waiter backs off with the slab,
then my fresh scrubs. Today, I'm a lacto-
vegetarian who lacks the stomach

for the seafood aisle. To think I would hover
at such a tank, holding my father's hand
as I selected my supper. Meanwhile, Mother's fingers,
daring, dive into barrels of salt-cured herring,
high blood pressure be damned. Between them:

three biopsies; radiation therapy (two rounds);
one heart attack leading to short-lived clinical
death; one artificial coma; one pacemaker;
one benign brain tumour; one shunt; one case
of sepsis; one splenectomy.

And those are just entremets. What hubris
makes me think that, opting for tofu,
I get to opt out? Consume what suffers.
You're not done; hold on, you've still got
your sea legs. That green gunk.

While your heart's still in it, old broad,
while you've still got the stomach, and butter,
dunk 'til that plate is as clean as your stone.

NINETY-ONE YEARS

for Murray Libman, 1917–2008

Strike while the iron's hot; so he thought best.
Here for his effects, I find Hollywood's glow.
Ninety-one years of life stowed in one chest,

while at Union Station, stand-ins take their rest,
newsboys trumpet dust and crops that won't grow.
Strike while the iron's hot; so he thought best.

A betting man, Grandfather liked to test
his luck at card tables; all at one go,
ninety-one years of life stowed in one chest.

Extras in fedoras and cloche hats jest.
Grandfather waits for the last train to show.
Strike while the iron's hot; so he thought best.

At sixteen, he knew which trains travelled west.
Hobos, shoe shiners. A trickster on furlough,
ninety-one years of life stowed in one chest.

The star leaps at his director's behest.
Grandfather on the ledge grows in sorrow.
Strike while the iron's hot; so he thought best.
Ninety-one years of life stowed in one chest.

SUNNYBROOK HOSPITAL, TORONTO

for Murray Libman, 1917–2008

Comfortable, sir? the nurse asked,
adjusting Grandfather's pillow under his head.
Never one to resist a kibitz, *I make a good living,*
he said. Mother combed out his knotted
hair while he read the sports page.

From the age of twenty, he'd Christianized
those dark curls with Brylcreem,
just like his Chaverim, his goodfellas.
He crooned the jingle to me in my cradle:
A little dab'll do ya. That follicles are now tested
for DNA and banned substances wouldn't
surprise him: a man's pate will always rat
him out. And so in old age he gave up
the pomade and went *au naturel,* his greying
Jewfro the reclaimed freeborn crown
of every self-made man and his bookie:

Who answered to Baruch and Sheldon.
Who drove Lincoln Continentals.
Who played gin rummy and mah-jong.
Who wore velour sweat suits and sandals.
Who dropped out of Harbord Collegiate.
Who toasted at Seders: "Next year in Manhattan."
Who, deploring the weight of their unshorn heads,
*   at Christie Pits in '33 and armed*
*   with lead pipes, battled the Hitlerites.*

Taking leave of his body, we laid hands upon
what remained of him, indivisible as ether.
In the cab home, the animal scent of unwashed
hair on our fingers.

And the theory! You couldn't move in their bedroom for the theory!

My mother's books on top of the dresser, buttressed by ferns: *Fat Is a Feminist Issue. Jonathan Livingston Seagull. Passages. Roots.*

The Joys of both *Cooking* and *Sex.*

My father's sock drawer: coins from the Old World. Nail clippers. Bullets in an old lozenge tin. Suppositories. Condoms, pre-tubal ligation.

Mother's sock drawer: queen-size pantyhose, reinforced toes. Bridge Mix. Chocolate-covered jujubes, murder on the teeth.

Said father to mother, *Wait in the car.* First recorded in '64. Parked outside Robarts Library on St. George. Said hero to maiden, *Wait in the car; I'll be back in a second.* December twilight. Engine off. Maiden rubs bare hands together, wishes for radio, *Look* magazine, Oh Henry! bar. Two hours later hero returns, unconcerned.

Anecdote explained to daughter. Question asked in emergency room, Saturday afternoon.

Answer: lady's fur-lined leather gloves. From Eaton's.

Father's fist breaks glass shower door. I take sister to neighbours. Orthodox Jews. Won't call an ambulance on the Sabbath.

To Father, Mother becomes pronoun with no antecedent. In other words, she's it.

It lawyers up.

Written from my one-bedroom apartment on what would have been your forty-third anniversary. A blessing on our three abodes.

INAUGURATION

Elijah's role as precursor continues in Jewish tradition,
with the development of messianic expectations;
at the Passover table a place is set for Elijah
in case he returns to inaugurate the messianic age.
—Richard J. Clifford

I.

I didn't want you to live in a world
without wonder, Mother said, by way of excuse.
Every spring I'd asked, *Was it you?*
Then, *Tell me the truth.* Credit her: she was good.
Indignant, even. *Why is it so hard to believe?*
I had to leave home before she'd confess.

Even the curtain blowing over the open window
was her. Certainly, the door slamming shut.
The nibbled corner of the matzo she'd shown
me before, as she placed it on his plate. The wine
in the silver-plated goblet from Montreal Judaica:
look at it, drained! What more did I need?

II.

Faith I asked.
Herself she gave.

III.

After the last Seder, rinsing out tinfoil
for reuse, she spoke of her first date with Father,
how just before curtain he'd leaned over (a kiss?)
and plucked her gold-plated earrings off;
Elijah seizing Jezebel's tribute to Baal.

IV.

Her Timing was as good as Her Word.

V.

Talk to her, says the nurse. She can still hear, I swear.

VI.

This can't be my life.

DISTANCE

Love lost to reading. Books, journals, even signs in the distance.
Playbills before curtain. The crowd at a distance.

Suppressing my embarrassment by withdrawing into print.
Hubris. As if I could disinherit distance.

O why did I sit with the straps of my purse binding my feet,
reading discounted books? Learning love at a distance.

I should have asked the time, unashamed to be unoccupied.
Or dared looking up and off into the distance.

WISH YOU WERE HERE

PRAGUE FUGUE
after A.M. Klein

Kindlers of ash, they cull husks to be
glassed, gather bones broken in far-ranging
places. They have bankers' boxes for pillows
and a private's rations.

How to keep hands steady while sorting
Hebraic motes, indexing echoes?
I picture them, when marble heads are turned,
filching from the relics displayed before us.

A speck from a *silver spice box, unembossed.*
A blue thread dangling from a *prayer shawl
for young boy, c. 1811.* A nail's worth of wax
from the dormant pit of a *menorah,
provenance doubtful.*

Smuggled under the tongue, a scrap
small enough to run any gauntlet will harden
into new enamel. For now, the throbbing
toothache of reprieve.

This is Holocaust industry, this anthem
composed for typewriter and index card.
Jews, are these your musicians?

WISH YOU WERE HERE

Bucharest

Woman in gentrified bookshop café
drinks oolong tea: eggshell cashmere top,
bobbed hair, smart shoes.

Opening a Taschen book on home décor,
she turns on her phone and photographs
each one of its pages.

London

Hotel in Paddington; dining room in basement.
Each morning a gunner fires toast at us.

Our rations: one pouch of black tea, one pat
of butter, one packet of jam, two of sugar.

We could afford to dine otherwise:
eggs and beans at the pub; French pastries
at the café with wing chairs and free papers.
But for the duration of our tour, we report
at seven for our free continental breakfast.
Dismal, yes. But how much more without us?

Paris Haiku

Under Pont Neuf bridge
A bed made on a stone ledge
Hospital corners

Toronto

The server brings a chair to your table,
straddles it backwards, warbles
the lower-case menu as if you're a bandmate.

But you can still find places where waitresses
bring your coffee and steak together,
both lukewarm, the cheque under the saucer.

The booze can above a bakery in Kensington.
One winter's dawn before I left, we improvised
a limbo bar with someone's lost muffler.

DOUBLE EXPOSURE

The child's blackness composed against
the white gauze bandage:

Searing, I say.

The man's black frame contrasted
with the white sheets, the whites of his
eyes inside the black face:

The contrast, I mean.

The photographer puts down his coffee,
admiring the gleam of cup, spoon,
and saucer, then tweaks the salt shaker
before speaking.

His family had just left him outside the hospital.

My water glass captures a needle of light
like a mercury thermometer spiking.

It's shocking how quickly they forget I'm there,
he says.

They must be used to it, I say.

He turns back the pages of his portfolio,
stabs the man's eye with his trigger finger:

I talked to him, he said. *I didn't take precautions.*
I saw fear in his eyes and I caught it.

Was your shutter, I ask, *the last*
earthly song he heard?

The photographer turns. I go in for the kill:
Anyone could have taken it.

He closes his portfolio, his colour recovered.
But you didn't, he says.

TAKE IT OR LEAVE IT

A long line shuffles past the framed photographs;
last day for *Ansel Adams at the AGO*.
Time is short, so it's highlights only.
To me, an iceberg's a broken tooth in a thinning sea.

New Mexico: cold shadow, parched stone.
The man near me whispers to his girlfriend,
Colossal. Mother asks, *Where are the people?*
A question I ask myself. No one
has photographed me since childhood.

Mother leading me to the museum store, ignoring
my tremors. I am enjoined, not for the first time,
to not make a scene. I tell Mother the tremors are gone
as she approaches a set of champagne flutes, priced to move.

Waiting for her taxi, Mother tells a story: she was
at the Glendale Cinema, eating liquorice allsorts;
one got stuck in her throat—then, the accepted cure
was to wallop the back. When that didn't work,
water was forced down, wetting mother's dress.

She heard someone ask for a doctor but by then
the gelatin had dissolved. She gulped and sighed
to applause. At last the curtain rose and in darkness,
Mother finished her candy. Her sweet tooth

had taken root right after I had: *Before you, I could
take it or leave it.* Mother's cure for sadness is too tall
for my kitchen cabinets, and my bachelor apartment doesn't
have a mantle. I set the glasses in a row on my windowsill.
Their lean bellies drink in the dusk.

GROUP THERAPY

Each of us, in turn, has to answer, in one word,
the question: *What are you feeling?*

In December no less, when it gets dark at four
and this classroom's been double-booked.

Another band of politicized marginals
prowls restless in the corridor

while we sit in the folding-chair circle, weighing
raw responses to *What are you feeling?*

No time for tracts or tea, or even free tampons.
No time for support; just our word.

Okay, says the first; *Fine*, says the second.
But soon, sidestepping the common:

Flat; *Round*; *Spiky*; *Vulvar*; and best of all, *Orange*.
Gurgles of laughter, like water

from a forgotten hose. Raised to please, be placid,
unseen, untroublesome, we view jokes

as propitiation. *Orange* is legit.
Pierced by cloves, a Saint Sebastian sacrificed

to a fomenting stock. A kitchen Molotov cocktail.
Christmas gift from simpler times? No time,

no time for metaphors. The facilitator submits
her word, *Proud*, and an injunction to spread

the word. We put on coats, make metallic
small talk, our words bottle caps scrounged

from a fountain. Dispersal is never simple.
Fraternizing outside the confines of our group,

while not forbidden, feels profane. Even those
conjoined by a subway ride soon fall in, approach

the station in patchwork single file, POWs
allowed one last smoke. My penance:

I once encountered our facilitator at Loblaws.
Her face, breached, out of context, over

a knoll of unseasonal lychees. Not a smile
or nod. I turned as if prodded toward

the bakery aisle, a family-sized tub of croutons
to reflect on. At each meeting, I debate broaching

the matter, requesting some doctrine. The world
outside is where we blaspheme, starting with our dreams

of each other. Tell Margaret I dreamt of her walking
in Paris. *What happened to your cane?* I asked.

No answer. I walk home, playing hangman
with the one word for what I am feeling.

KINGDOM FUNGI

He who lies on the ground cannot fall
—Yiddish proverb

Wilhelm Marr, German nutbar,
first coined the term *antisemite* in 1879,
explains our guest scholar.

Jews had popped up all over Mitteleuropa
like poisonous mushrooms in living
forests, and Marr's compatriots
kept mistaking secular ones for more
delectable straw. Proof: the Roman Emperor
Claudius, conferrer of Israelite rights,
was himself felled by a toadstool
taken for a truffle.

To wit, a cartoon currently on exhibit
at Theresienstadt: a mushroom sporting
a hooked nose beneath a red and white
spotted bonnet. Caption: *Jews, like fungi,*
sprout in any patch of muck; thrive on dying
vegetation. Fooling amateur and connoisseur
alike with their toxic mimicry.

O when the time comes, let my renascence
be fungal: toadstool or truffle, my pick
of 2,300 genera. Hooked-nose optional.
I'll take my place in the fairy ring, as parasite
or hunted delicacy. White of an artist's fungus,
used for etchings the seduced will come see.

No, let me trumpet black destruction,
a marauding muscarine angel wearing my death
cap jauntily. Or let me at least induce jaundice,
just once. Morel or earth-star? Hallucinogenic
outlaw? Divine priest of Zoroastrian visions?
A contributor to sacred urine? Perhaps sign up
with the genus *bracket*? Heart rot's their racket.

O when the time comes, let my renascence
be fungal: toadstool or truffle, my pick
of 2,300 genera. Then as now, I'll be mostly water.

I'LL START TOMORROW

If you had just been a bigger person. Not as you are,
neither fat nor thin, forever stifling metabolic mutiny.
Openly zaftig you should have been, not hiding
your ass behind a cardigan. A flag folded over a coffin.
Here lies what Eastern European winters bequeathed her.

Either parade those log-cabin thighs, meant to stride
the Carpathian Mountains, or emulate the St. Médard girls,
eight hundred in all, who crawled to that church to beg
for tongue piercings to obliterate taste, for twenty-five-
pound weights to crush the longing in their chests,

for iron combs to tear their flesh. Pain that voluptuous
knows no bounds. Breasts battered and heads down
they heard the nuns meowing in ecstasy. On to their feast:
live coals swallowed whole, followed by leather-bound
copies of the New Testament. For forty days after

they lived on air sipped from spoons, then held their breath.
Who am I fooling? After giving birth, my mother mistook
me for a loaf of sourdough bread; instructed the nurse
not to slice me too thinly.

CEASEFIRE

So I look like one of Ingres' harem bathers
wearing leggings and sneakers, jogging
toward you. But do I deserve you telling me
that the Dairy Queen is behind me?

To what citadel will you retreat once
you've taken us fat women down? How
will you fill the sudden void? By seeking
relief from spoonable solids? More
of you to love, man on the street.

Come, race-walk beside us. Admit
you'll bawl when we've fallen
and the jogging tracks reek of gunpowder
and scorched sugar. 'Til then, man on the street,
we'll share our gluten-free rations.

ROSALIND FRANKLIN IN OPEN-TOE SANDALS

Her bare legs and open-toe platform pumps
are what you notice last in the photograph
of the young crystallographer at the conference.

First her hair, dark and loose. Then her smile.
The blouse open at the throat. Even in black
and white you can tell she's still tanned

from hiking the Alps. She is on our right,
about to open the door. The men on the left
are next, in shadow, but then Rosalind's

on the first step, and in their light. Nine years
before she dies, she has come to Lyon
from Paris where she works for fellow Jew

Mering at his convivial lab: a different photo
shows her in checked shirtwaist, hair in a loose
chignon, holding two petri dishes full

of the coffee they brewed in beakers.
How could she not see the structure of DNA
was a spiral staircase for inbred debutantes

to descend? How could she not spot
the base pairs, reproducing without end,
facing each other like inverted mirrors?

Photograph #51, the first glimpse of DNA's helix.
Rosalind took it with the same X-ray machine
she had used in Paris. When she saw that X-ray

of her ovarian tumour, it seemed benign
in comparison. But for that day in the Lyonnais sun,
England behind her, foot on the first rung.

YOUR WOMEN ARE BEAUTIFUL

Departure day: waiting for the airport
shuttle, I'm given a card for my comments.
Under "Please rate your stay at our resort"
I give the highest praise man can impart
on a place strange in climate and spirit:

Your women are beautiful. Boarding the plane,
I sort the crucial factors. Did some viceroy
spike their genic punch bowl with his seed?
What about those flavourful weeds in their salads?
Whatever wonder it is, we could use it

in Edmonton. I smuggle past customs a specimen
of indigent citrus fruit. The girl who gave me
this one said they grew wild near her house.
I canvassed her home one hot afternoon, a simple
hut made of the local wood. What they say is true:

untroubled by progress, these good people
speak from the heart, don't bother with riddles.
(I know how that sounds. *I want you,* she said.
I liked that she had nowhere to be.) Welcome home:
someone's shitting on the lawn my condo board

calls the park. The taxi drives off; the man rises
and now I see what I took for a wetsuit is hair,
brown and thick as fur. His eyes roll as he whimpers
at me; no, *for* me, in my guayabera and jeans.
He grunts and snorts, moving closer.

I stay still, let him sniff me. He tastes my skin,
I taste him: banana. He shakes his head, inspecting
my loins: unlike his, mine's a light blue streak,
the sky killing drought. He joins me on the ground,
my smuggled fruit a coin in his hand.

IF I HAD YOUR COCK

I would use it as a mail opener, paperweight,
    Tetris partner
Emotional sundial

Put up your picture with it
Cheat on my taxes with it
Grind pills, pigment and spices with it
and it goes without saying,
    I would shoot pool with it

Start fires with it
Write my name with it
Cross my Ts and dot my Is with it
Carry old men's shopping bags with it
Shoehorn my good pumps on with it

and rolling out dough with it
would offer you a selection:
plain, chocolate or cinnamon
Then I'd figure out some way
    to floss with it

Never hesitate to mention it
        in polite conversation
Use it casually, formally, lovingly, disdainfully
Point out shooting stars with it
Look at porn on the net with it

Go to market, displaying my merchandise on it
My standard unit of measurement
Sterling standard
Star sheaf in our nation's bread basket

Hang our dirty laundry, grey and weeping on it
        while I rest my feet on it
Stirring a G and T on it
and write you this poem
        in invisible ink

ROLL CALL

A is for Adonis who logged in as Weekend Daddy.

B is for Bacchus who swore he'd quit if we had a baby.

C is for Cupid who lived on a boat on blocks.

D is for Daedalus who picked my bike lock.

E is for Ether who was a Unitarian Rasta.

F is for Faunus who proposed (to stay in Canada).

G is for Geryon who said, *Two words: join a gym.*

H is for Heracles who knows this poem is about him.

I is for Ixion who used ashes for soap.

J is for Jove who used his webcam to grope.

K is for Kronos who gave Daedalus my PIN.

L is for Lycaon who counselled taking it on the chin.

M is for Momus who liked to drunk-dial.

N is for Neptune who swam off with Kyle.

O is for Orestes who blamed his dead mother.

P is for Pan who lived in her Chrysler.

Q is for Quirinus who asked why I just couldn't listen.

R is for Remus whose bro shanked him in prison.

S is for Silenus who couldn't do or teach.

T is for Tantalus who cruised girls out of our reach.

U is for Ulysses who said, *It doesn't count if it's head.*

V is for Vulcanus who burned down my tool shed.

W is for Walter who said I couldn't go further.

X is for Xuthus who made an ass out of Walter.

Y is for YHWH who couldn't pick up a phone.

Z is for Zeus who says, *For our sakes, just die alone.*

WONDER

On offer at the public market near the Duomo,
a dog mounts a woman from behind. On all fours,
she appears as resigned as the Virgin on that fresco
near my hotel. The illicit magazine costs thirteen
euros and comes shrink-wrapped in plastic.

Or does the signor want a genuine Florentine
leather vest? Postcard? Three sets of female buttocks,
caked in golden sand like milkless polenta above
the tourist's taunt: *Wish you were here.* This signora
wants some other era, of signs and wonders.

Not the bar at the Intercontinental in Old Montreal,
where the speciality is absinthe minus the fairies.
I've pledged to meet Jeff there tonight for half-price
drinks during *cinq à sept.* Jeff got what he calls
my details from a networking site I joined years ago.

Just passing through for work, he pulled up my profile,
thought he'd shoot me an email. *See you at five,*
I replied. *Sincerely.* A link to *Kama Sutra: The Sensual
Arts* soon appeared in my inbox. Sorcery, no doubt.
Then, from the American Board of Sexology came

a wondrous notice: *Jeff thought you might like this.*
It's eleven at night in Florence. I'm drinking Chianti,
alone at the counter, watching two men debate
in great depth the slicing of ham. With darting fingers
they demonstrate the requisite breadth while Jeff

awaits the redhead with the tattoo of a winged pig
on her shoulder. On her rear, she's inked her mantra:
Wish you were here. This signora wants some other
epoch, one with sighs and wonders, not a hard sell.
Some writing on my city's ramparts, faith in spells.

POSTERITY

Is it just my imagination,
or do I really need to put on
my bra in order to write?

Girls, pull in those lies!
A pen in my mouth lest I bite
my tongue when the whip
comes down.

I wear heels, too. The hobbling
sort. Before they make me run,
I'll demand a head start.

Palm fronds may wave in Poland,
but don't tell me some things
don't change. This one's
for posterity.

Posterity, you say? A long walk
off a short pier. Better to stay
in the car, bra in my mouth.

RETOUCHED

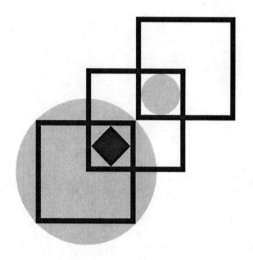

FROM SPANISH MADE EASY (MARIA HAS A DATE)

We lunch together at an empty table,
the waiter bending like a sunflower
while Rodrigo's peas, my plate of beans,
our beer and *leche* appear in a subsequent
panel, arrayed like tarot cards, and neatly
detailed. Rodrigo pays the *cuenta* from a fat
wad of pesos, leaving a liberal *propina*
for the black-jacketed *camarero*. After
work we meet at the disco. Rodrigo has
his shirt open to his navel. I dance, alone,
under the mirror ball, while he hums "Te Amo."
The hem of my skirt flips up, matching
my hairdo, a pageboy confection. Set into bed
and smiling, saintly, I am trapped, as always,
in a room without walls, without doorways
or windows, a simple T stands for my bedside
table. Tomorrow, I will consult an atlas:
it is no shame to admit to a stranger I am lost,
Estoy perdida, and beg for direction.

RETOUCHED

Fate, destiny, kismet: none
seem adequate to capture
the coincidence, this sudden
appearance of the picture
in the shop window
showcasing my failure.
Myself on my wedding day.

I follow my bright gaze:
it appears I'm intended for the dive
across the way. My skin
has been retouched, the veneer
a tone I'll call *golem*.
How many years since

I was wed? Roughly a thousand.
The groom's now gotten away,
South America or Iceland.
So the photographer has me
to display his skill with lenses
and light metres? Slow trade

on this street, where nerves
are frayed by sneakers tied
to hydro poles. Unlike me,
my portrait has company:
teenaged boys point at Torah
scrolls while babies loll

on their bellies. I am the only
bride, made to stand on her stool,
naughty girl, until the bell rings.
Unfettered by any backdrop,
I've been composed like a pyramid
of gleaming apples. That smile

will never develop into a laugh.
So I laugh for me. All night
my window is lit up to highlight
my spoken-for cleavage,
bared yet beigely modest.
But no lout's hoot will ever

raise my tender head. The silver
part in my hair: the path
of a small craft through calm water.
Cool virgin, at last I am insured
against floods and fire,
rioting and plunder.

PRAYER FOR THE HEADLESS BOAR

Must you dawdle in the Jewish ghetto?
The gates were locked at both ends each dusk;
you may want to catch up to the group.

That plaque dedicated to victims
of *hitlérienne* violence? What should it matter
to you if the others can't spare it a moment?

Sip Pouilly-Fumé by the dolphin monument.
Nibble *biscuits navette* freckled with fennel seeds,
fished from fake barrels, their texture like cartilage

while in a peripheral vision a black boar sways
gently in the butcher's window. *Seigneur,*
try not to lose it—gather your wits and gewgaws

to bring home while the headless boar hangs
by its paws in that light like chamomile tea.
The palm trees glow a bit red every now and then

but you're on holiday. Why spoil it for the others.
Just because, before Vieux Nice, you never tasted
an apéritif, or knew Hitler was an adjective.

PINS AND NEEDLES

You're as heavy as a cow's tongue,
eyeless, disjointed; half-awake, I rock you
with my right arm. Sleeping falcon,
I'll shimmy your hood off though it hurts
to feel your nerves stir. Unless you stay flaccid
like this, muscle memory anesthetised.
Never will you not play piano again. Quicken,
and your *qwerts* won't be wasted on poems
about sleeping limbs but on a whole suite
about shipping live fish in Greece, two weeks
of fish pens and that French trucker, fucking
him on the road from Sète to Crete, told
in lines sticky as dashboard ass. Right-handed
I am, but evil one, you know my heart.

GAME

The most French Frenchman I ever met—
after that man in striped wife-beater and blue
beret drawing caricatures on the Promenade
des Anglais, red scarf tied 'round his fat neck.
Didier ate dessert with baguette, longed
for coquilles St. Jacques and the lavender

fires of Sète. His name for me was *La petite*.
Une belle huitre, he'd say, hacking up phlegm.
A pretty oyster I've made. He taught me to hold
a champagne flute by the stem, to eat cheese
at room temperature only, to taste *la mer*
in a raw sea urchin.

Didier liked to shit with the door open,
greeting each splash with, *Ça porte de bonheur!*
When he asked, *Tu fais les petits cacas,*
où les gros cacas? I had no words.
Didier, by his own admission, had been
denied by the teeth and hair fairies; balding,

he wore rimless glasses, and badly needed
crowns. Before sleep each night, he slathered
cold cream on his face and scalp. If he lived
to forty, he would sail away on his boat. *What
about me, should I be so lucky?* Red wine
aggravated his hemorrhoids

but he taught me to turn the bottle as I poured
so none of it would spill. Our first night
in his truck, he squatted in the cabin, pants down,
grimacing. Closing the windshield
curtains, he said the last woman he'd been with
had thrust her finger up his ass,

fissuring his anus. His asshole, therefore,
was off-limits, but for anything else
he was game. With my ass on his dashboard;
his freshly creamed head between my knees:
Une belle huitre, he said to me.

Didier's truck was as hard and unadorned as his body.
No crucifixes or decals, no amulets to ward off evil
eyes and accidents. Small fridge built into the console
between seats, and a red curtain separating the front seats
from the bunk beds in the back.

In the glove compartment: a road atlas of Europe,
a harmonica and two editions of *Que-sais je?*,
the Gallic autodidacts' preferred paperback.
Didier's topics: *Histoire du Canada* and *L'humour
juif*. On the fly-leaf he's written, *Woody Allen*.

Like my fellow exchange teachers, I rented a studio,
slept on a pull-out sofa the French call a *clic-clac*,
Didier said, for the reproachful sound it made
when assembled. Didn't a professor (in Nice!) deserve
a bed? *Peu importe* if it's just two semesters!

Didier made me write down my monthly stipend
while he checked the tanks. He returned with dark
patches of damp on his anorak, glosses fogged up.
I was oppressed, he said, as he adjusted driver
and passenger seats to face each other.

A high school dropout, Didier outclassed me
in salary. I agreed; he shuffled the cards. The overhead
light glowed, amber and warm. I told Didier
I didn't know how to play. He looked up from his hand
to say, *But I haven't even told you which game.*

THE FERRY

Take what you need for the night, Didier says,
cleaning his good shoes. I climb down from the cabin
to find a procession of professional mourners.
Black-robed widows tailgate a coffin, moans
mingling with the truckers' multi-lingual calls
to each other. Then cement becomes claret and gold
carpeting. Didier's told me there's a disco onboard
and two restaurants, fine dining and casual.
Truckers in denim and leather emerge from the garage,
swarm the check-in, workboots trampling *fleurs-de-lys*.
Room cards in hand, they converge on the lounge.
My first time drinking on water. Truckers slouch
on vinyl banquettes beneath chandeliers. Didier orders
Jack Daniel's; for me, white wine, chilled.

Smells of tobacco, sweat, lighter fluid. The bar
stools, upholstered in fake whale foreskins, are tested.
A couple, backpackers, observe me from the far shore
of this smoking sea of work-worn men aged nineteen
to sixty. The man drinks beer, his woman kir royale.
I recognize their edition of *Greece on a Shoestring*,
the same white stone church against the same blue sea.
Didier chooses this moment to show off his trick
of crushing a beer can against his brow. The woman
elbows the man, who searches his backpack for a phone.
Calling Interpol, I'm sure, to report a victim of sex
trafficking. *In her twenties, Southern or Eastern European.
Or Roma, based on her colouring. No obvious signs
of abuse, well-fed, but clearly exhausted.*

CUL DE SAC

In France, Didier says, the roads are smooth
as glass. The autostrade are something else.
Destinations painted on the asphalt in large
white letters: *San Remo, Imperia, Genoa.*
As we approach, the letters stretch 'til they snap
and are gone. A hallucination. Didier drives

through tunnels blasted into mountains,
no illumination but from his headlights,
past hillside towns I still dream of years later.
We stop for cappuccino; Didier swirls
his cup, gathering the cream from the bottom.
All in the wrist, he says. Before leaving,

I buy pasta shaped like bicycle wheels,
the spokes red, white and green, knowing
I will never dare eat it. In the cab,
Didier pushes a button above the dash,
ejecting a paper disc. A register of the kilometres
he's travelled that day.

Other truckers drive further than the threshold
enforced by *les flics*, but not him.
He pulls up to the side of the road and we share
dinner: sausage coins on biscuits.
Didier wipes his Swiss army knife clean,
wipes clean the tray that served as our table.

He sings along to Renaud as he slides
the little fridge back into place. We shake out
the mats, brush down the seats, then brush
our teeth in the gas station. Didier says
his boat's nearly seaworthy. He watches me
swallow my birth control pill.

Do I remember our meeting in Toledo last month?
Do I recall what Didier said?

Lying awake on my clic-clac, I mapped
my escape: train to Saint Sebastian, bus
to Madrid, then Segovia and Toledo
to stroll the Jewish ghettoes. The desk clerk
at my hotel gave me the grapes. At midnight,
as fireworks exploded over the plaza,
I was to eat all twelve for luck.

Only nineteen Europeans do your job, I respond.
I've earned my reward: face time with the cargo.

I remember the clerk, smiling when I returned
with Didier, letting us grope each other in his lobby.
The same man who the day before had drawn me
a map to the Jewish museum now upgraded me
to a cleaner room and slipped me a condom.
Grateful I was for his blessing.

Outside Ancona, Didier pulls over. He changes
into rubber overalls, pulls on work gloves and waders,
the helmet with lamp attached.

He zips me into his anorak, adjusts the hood,
then pinches my ass. I follow him
to the three black tanks hitched to his truck,
slick with rainwater. Didier helps me climb the steps
to the top. He pries the first lid open,
readies the oxygen.

Sea bass, worth sixty thousand euros each.
One of each sex. Tranquilized. Bred to breed.

All I see is dark water. Didier confides: this unloading
will be his first of its kind. He's used to transporting
offspring, thousands of fry per tank.

A risk-free unburdening: just point a hose and *whoosh*,
out they come, miniscule blobs. He's expected
to lose some.

To unload these beasts, he'll have to descend
into the tank to grasp each ten-kilogram fish.
Lose his grip and it's back to hauling dead livestock.

Didier shows me a prospectus, a gift
from a Turkish ichthyologist he met on his last haul.
I'm to translate the lingo of fish husbandry,
English to French. *Genotyping. Brood stock.*
Mariculture: aquaculture occurring in saltwater.
La petite must earn her keep, starting with *sea louse.*

SOFT

The men who work the fish farms are soft,
Didier says. Not like their grandfathers,
casting off in fishing rigs before first light.

He shows me the scars shaped like parentheses
running along to his spine, raised and pink.
The accident, he says, wasn't his fault.

Pinned beneath a dead bull weighing
a thousand kilograms, he shouldn't have lived.
The first surgery took six hours.

The cabin is what it is, nothing more.
Everything bolted down; shower stall and toilet
in unsettling proximity.

I turn on the radio console to Celine Dion.
A wheelchair, says Didier.
The ship's engines compete with *La Dion*.

Didier's obligatory military service
was less precarious than his life on the road.
In Zagreb, his commander

invited the unit to a local brothel.
But first Didier phoned his girlfriend
to ask her blessing.

With what wonder Didier regards me
when I ask if she gave it. Once in Montreal,
a man tried to drag me into an alley.

I pushed him off, made bold by morning
light and traffic. Because I was naked,
because Didier said it as if grasping

the punchline to a joke
in some film that had always confused him,
I left him smoking in the lower bunk,

and put on my dress. At the disco
a Croatian trucker buys me gin fizzes.
He's escorting me to my cabin

when I see Didier. He is in his anorak
reflected in the mirrored walls lining the staircase.
Earlier I'd wished him an early death

for claiming that if I'd had an inkling of real life
I'd be better in bed. That was my problem,
a life confined like a calf;

that, and eating between meals.
Features still softened by sleep, Didier
wakes each night to tend to his cargo,

walks his bow-legged walk
caused by three spinal surgeries. Pity floods
the pews of my heart like light

through a stained-glass window. I thank
Dado, then trail Didier to the garage,
already cold in my hot dress and sandals.

UNLOADED

What do I know of the sea?

The Rime of the Ancient Mariner. Odysseus. Poseidon and his Trident. Depleted. Or teeming. Migrants turned away, drowned and lost. Pleasure cruisers rescued by coast guard. Arctic ice floes. *The Tempest.* Prospero. Pearl and abalone divers. Bathyspheres. Slave ships and Jacques Cousteau. The bends.

What do I know of Kalymnos?

A blister of land near Turkey. Sunrise at Pothia, the port. Didier drives the truck uphill. Narrow road lined with one-storey houses and wild roses. Old women, unconcerned, emerge with market baskets, frozen until we pass. A road chiselled out of bare rock. In the distance, black livestock scattered on rounded hills: poppy seeds on a bagel. Didier points his truck seaward. Tires bounce so hard I levitate, ass clearing the seat. In the bay, pens of pipe and nylon netting: underwater tennis courts. A playground for women doped on hormones.

What do I know of mermen?

Didier afraid to let go. Didier looking towards me, pointing my camera at him. Sorcerer, shaman. We have caught him mid-ritual. Fish bucks between my lover's knees like an enraged dog unleashed before a fight. Fish in flight, pewter skin but fins and gills tinged a scar-tissue pink. Comically downturned mouth, sunk in discontent. More comedy: the men scurry back and forth, back and forth. Fish eclipses the sun, then hits its mark. Queer deposit: fish released to unleash havoc of forced mating, pre-programmed and out of season.

What do I know of heartache?

That it has no season. That at first it's physical, like the bends.

LAST NIGHT THEY WERE GODS

For they dined at communal tables, busboys
rushing to refill water goblets and baskets of bread,
their voices a babel of Indo-European languages.

Gobshite, the blue-eyed Tunisian from Marseilles
echoed, to the Brits' delight. Didier lifted a buttock
and farted. *Good lad*, said the cork-sniffing Scotsman.

When Piraeus approached, the men retraced their steps
to slump inside their cabs. In the kitchen, the waiters
rolled the linen tablecloths, and drowned them in bleach.

NOTES & ACKNOWLEDGEMENTS

The poem "Inauguration" refers to the Jewish tradition of setting a place for the Prophet Elijah at the Passover table should he return to inaugurate the messianic age.

Previous versions of poems from this book have appeared in *Arc Poetry Magazine*, *The New Quarterly*, *Matrix*, *The Malahat Review*, *The Literary Review of Canada*, *The Dalhousie Review*, *EVENT*, *OVS*, *Touchstone*, *Soliloquies*, *Ozone Park*, *The Nashwaak Review*, *Kestrel*, *The Orange Coast Review*, *Existere*, *The Emerson Review*, *Canadian Ginger*, *I Found It at the Movies: An Anthology of Film Poems* and *Best Canadian Poetry in English 2010*. Thank you to the editors of each.

My deepest gratitude to the teachers who first nurtured many of these poems: A.F. Moritz, David Donnell, George Elliott Clarke and Jacob Scheier.

Everyone at Nightwood Editions, including Amber McMillan and Silas White for the thoughtful editing, Carleton Wilson for the perfect cover art, and Nathaniel Moore for support and encouragement.

Everyone at Artscape Toronto and the Gibraltar Point Centre for the Arts.

My partner, Emmanuel Nault.

ABOUT THE AUTHOR

Rebecca Păpucaru lives in the Eastern Townships, Quebec. She was a finalist for the Penguin Random House Canada Student Award for Fiction (2004) and *Arc Poetry Magazine* Poem of the Year Contest (2002). Her poetry has appeared in the anthologies *I Found It at the Movies: An Anthology of Film Poems* (2014) and *The Best Canadian Poetry in English* (2010). *The Panic Room* is her first book of poetry.

PHOTO CREDIT: EMMANUEL NAULT